Erik SATIE

Socrate

Drame Symphonique

Vocal Score
Klavierauszug

SERENISSIMA MUSIC, INC.

CONTENTS

I. Portrait de Socrate — 3

II. Les bords de l'Ilissus — 17

III. Mort de Socrate — 37

CHARACTERS

Alcibiades	Soprano
Socrates	Mezzo-Soprano
Phaedrus	Soprano
Phaedo	Mezzo-Soprano

(all four roles are usually taken by a single voice)

Duration: ca. 30 minutes

Premiere: April, 1918
Paris, Salon of Princess Edmond de Polignac
Jane Bathori, vocal solo / Erik Satie, piano

ISBN: 1-932419-73-X
This score is a slightly modified unabridged reprint of the
score published in 1919 by Éditions de la Sirène, Paris, plate E.D. 2 L.S.
The score has been enlarged to fit the present format.

Printed in the USA
First Printing: January, 2009

à Madame la Princesse Edmond de POLIGNAC

SOCRATE
Drame Symphonique en 3 Parties avec Voix
Sur des dialogues de Platon traduits par Victor Cousin

ERIK SATIE

I. PORTRAIT DE SOCRATE
(LE BANQUET)

SERENISSIMA MUSIC, INC.

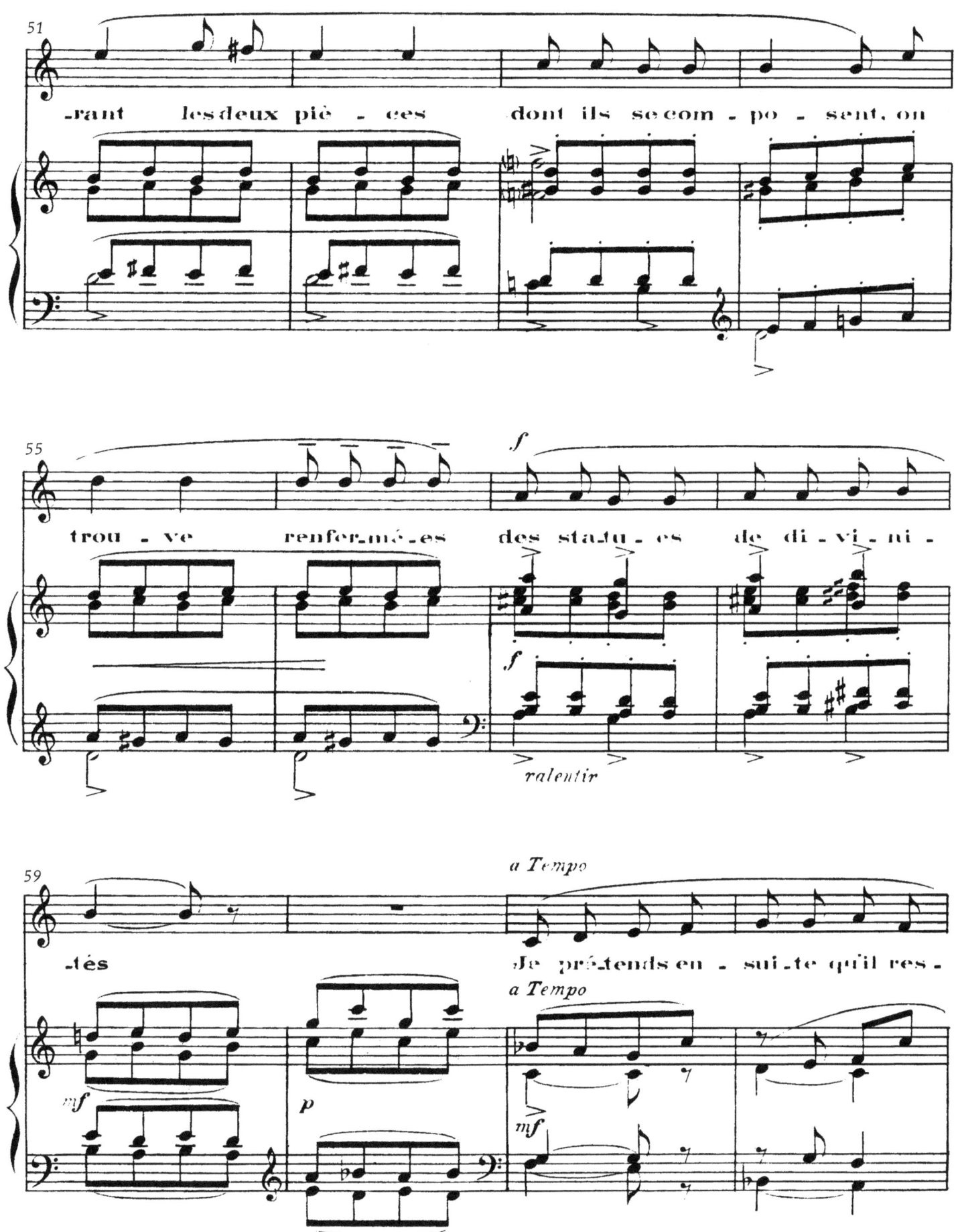

16

II. BORDS DE L'ILISSUS
(PHEDRE)

20

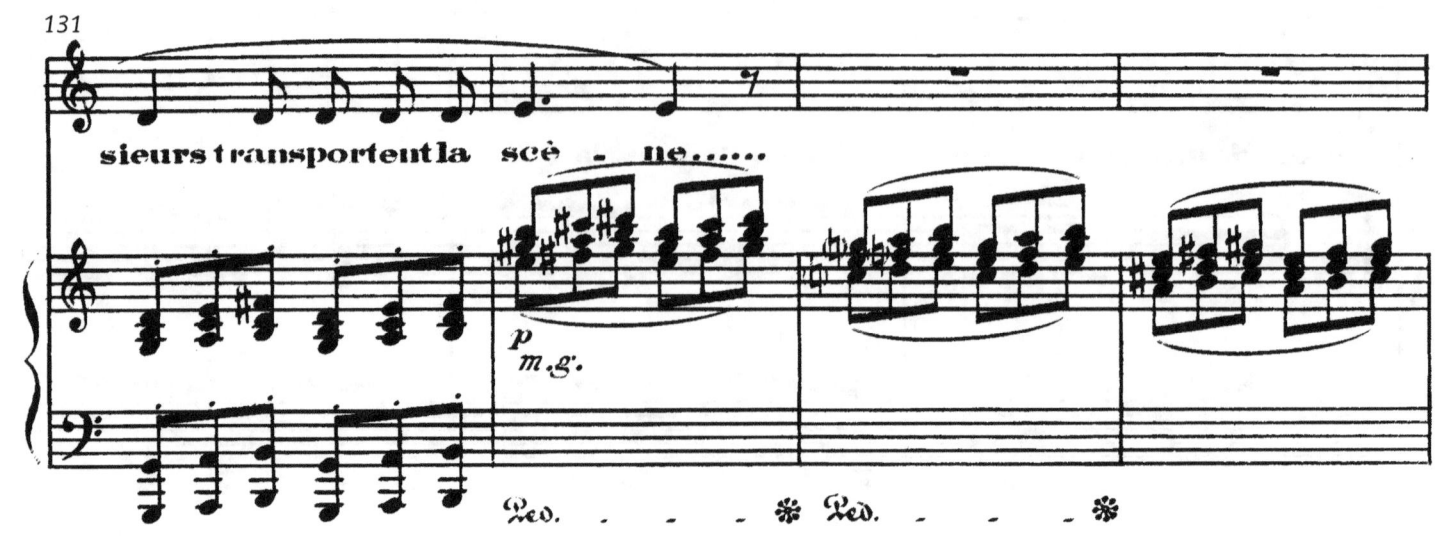
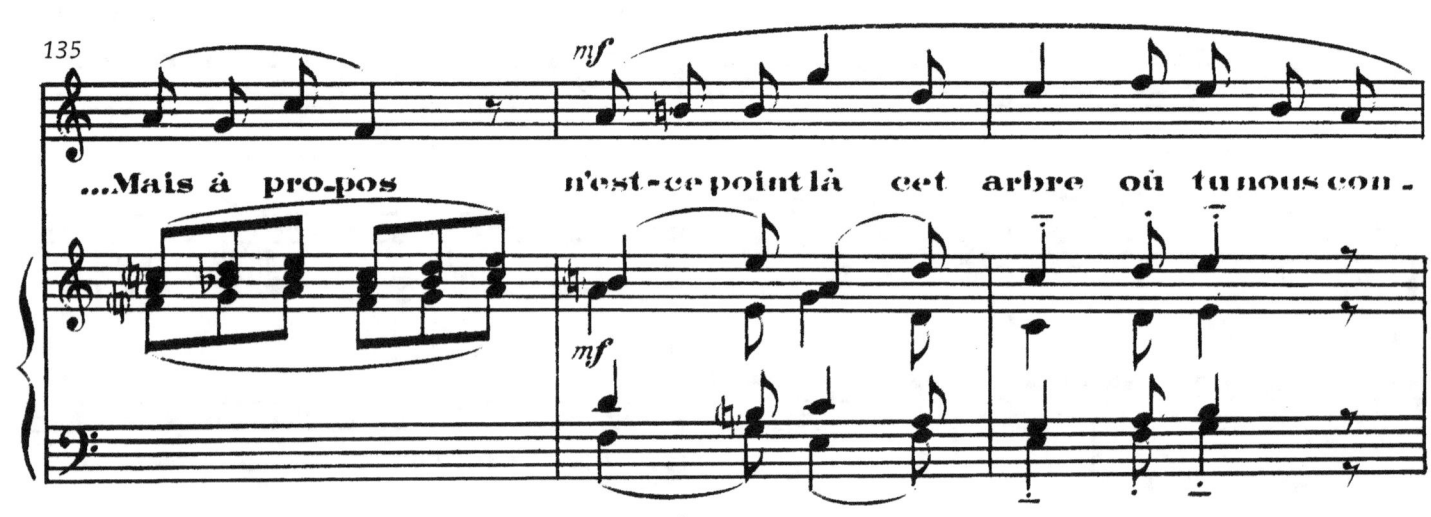

176
pp
-res et ces sta - tu - es.
Goûte un peu l'air
p
pp
180
ppp
qu'on y respi - re:
est - il rien de plus suave et de si dé -
ppp
184
mf subito
-li-ci-eux?
Le chant des ci - ga - les a quelque cho -
mf subito

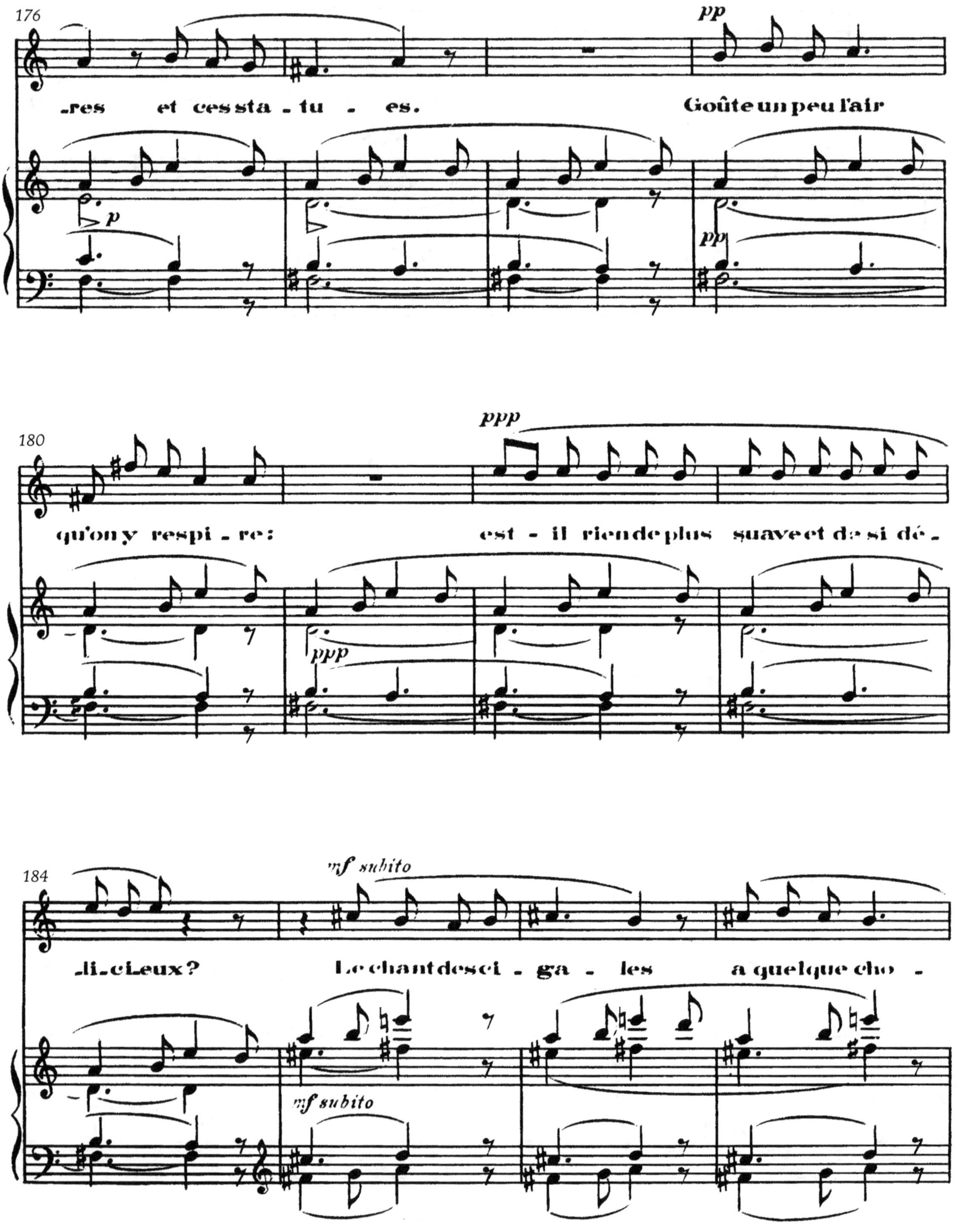

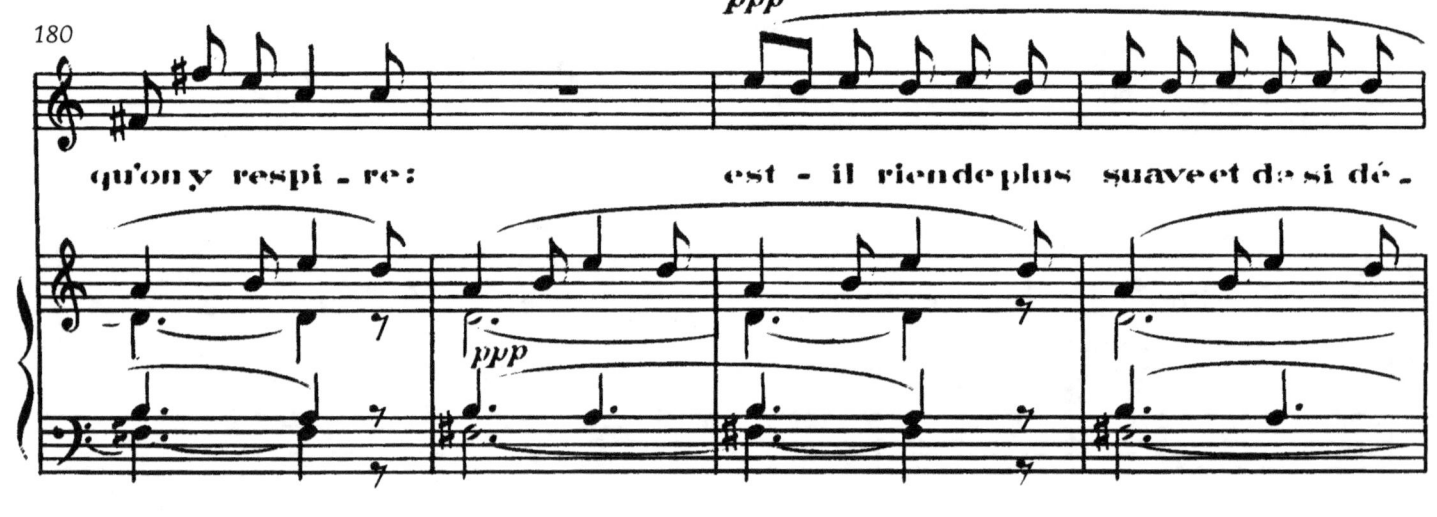

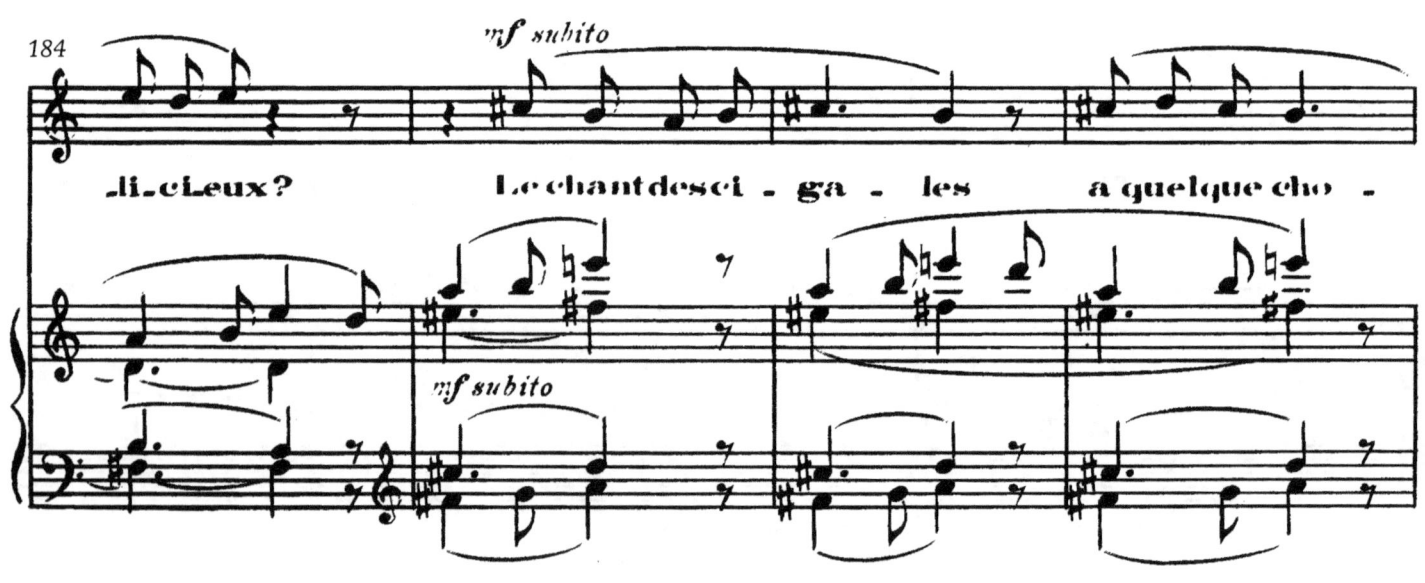

III. MORT DE SOCRATE
(PHÉDON)

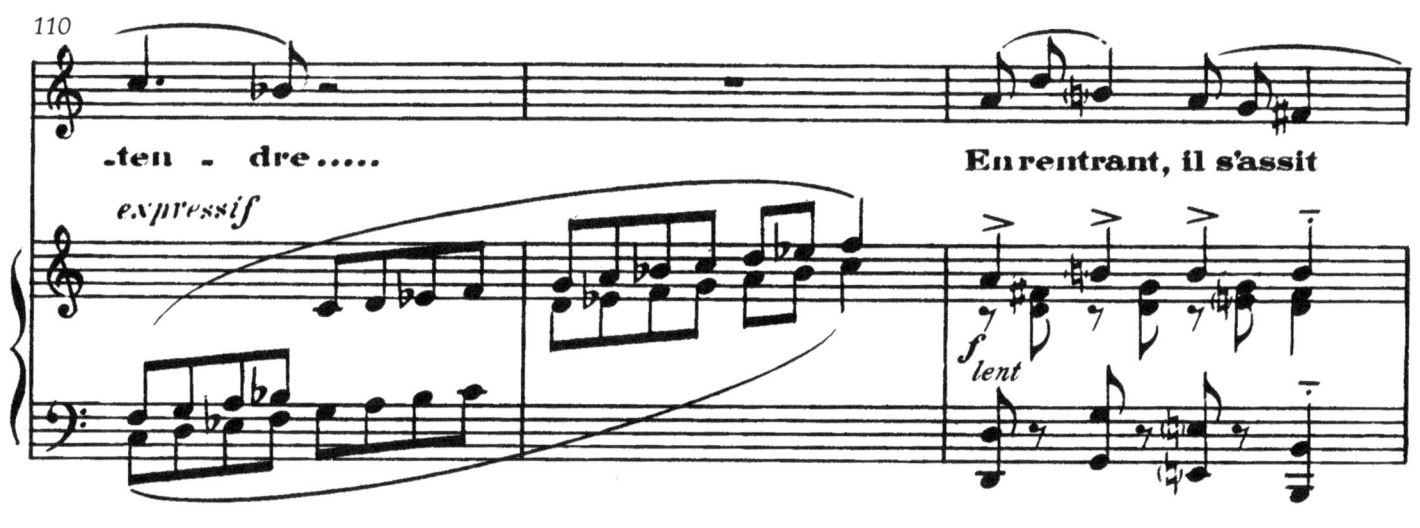

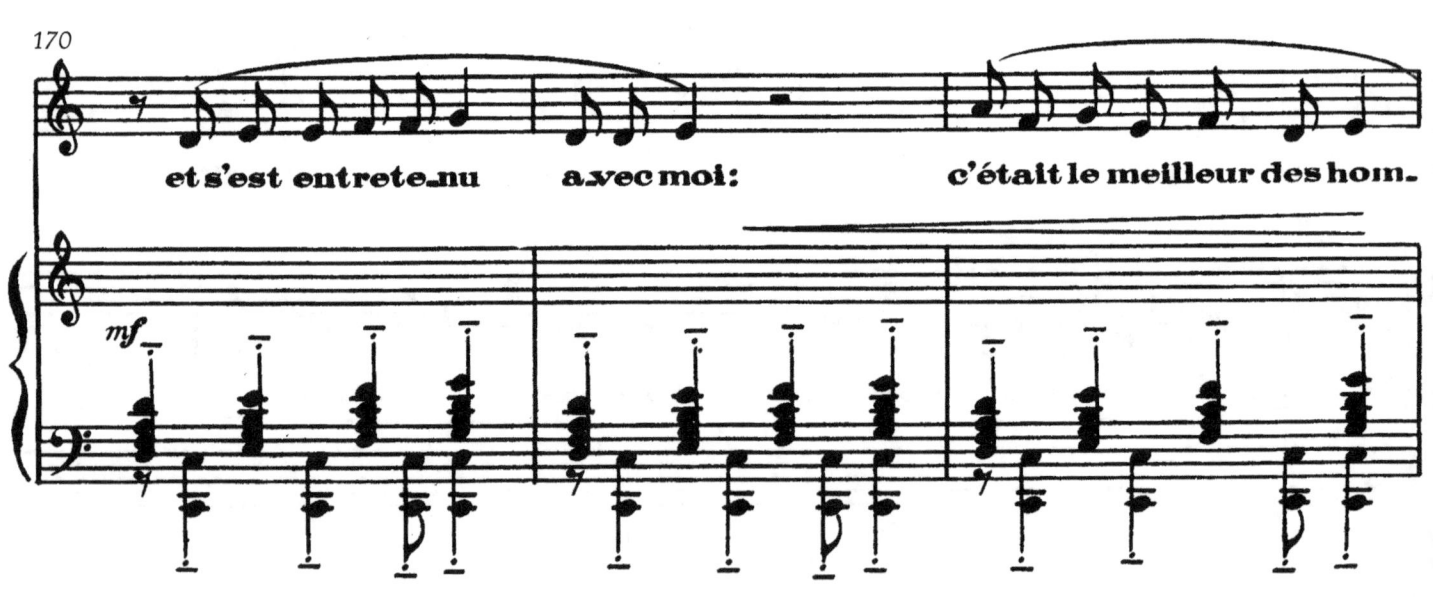

I. Portrait of Socrates
from *Symposium*, 32-33-35

Alcibiades

And now, my boys, I shall praise Socrates in a figure which will appear to him to be a caricature, and yet I speak, not to make fun of him, but only for the truth's sake. I say, that he is exactly like the busts of Silenus, which are set up in the statuaries' shops, holding pipes and flutes in their mouths; and they are made to open in the middle, and have images of gods inside them. I say also that he is like Marsyas the satyr. And are you not a flute-player? That you are, and a performer far more wonderful than Marsyas. He indeed with instruments used to charm the souls of men by the power of his breath, and the players of his music do so still: for the melodies of Olympus are derived from Marsyas who taught them. But you produce the same effect with your words only, and do not require the flute: that is the difference between you and him. And if I were not afraid that you would think me hopelessly drunk, I would have sworn as well as spoken to the influence which they have always had and still have over me. For my heart leaps within me more than that of any Corybantian reveller, and my eyes rain tears when I hear them. And I observe that many others are affected in the same manner. And this is what I and many others have suffered from the flute-playing of this satyr.

Socrates

You praised me, and I in turn ought to praise my neighbor on the right.

II. On the banks of the Ilissus
from *Phaedrus*, 4-5

Socrates

Let us turn aside and go by the Ilissus; we will sit down at some quiet spot.

Phaedrus

I am fortunate in not having my sandals, and as you never have any, I think that we may go along the brook and cool our feet in the water; this will be the easiest way, and at midday and in the summer is far from being unpleasant.

Socrates

Lead on, and look out for a place in which we can sit down.

Phaedrus

Do you see the tallest plane-tree in the distance?

Socrates

Yes.

Phaedrus

There are shade and gentle breezes, and grass on which we may either sit or lie down.

Socrates

Move forward.

Phaedrus

I should like to know, Socrates, whether the place is not somewhere here at which Boreas is said to have carried off Orithyia from the banks of the Ilissus?

Socrates

Such is the tradition.

Phaedrus

And is this the exact spot? The little stream is delightfully clear and bright; I can fancy that there might be maidens playing near.

Socrates

I believe that the spot is not exactly here, but about a quarter of a mile lower down, where you cross to the temple of Artemis, and there is, I think, some sort of an altar of Boreas at the place.

Phaedrus

I have never noticed it; but I beseech you to tell me, Socrates, do you believe this tale?

Socrates

The wise are doubtful, and I should not be singular if, like them, I too doubted. I might have a rational explanation that Orithyia was playing with Pharmacia, when a northern gust carried her over the neighbouring rocks; and this being the manner of her death, she was said to have been carried away by Boreas. According to another version of the story she was taken from Areopagus, and not from this place. But let me ask you, friend: have we not reached the plane-tree to which you were conducting us?

Phaedrus

Yes, this is the tree.

Socrates

By Here, a fair resting-place, full of summer sounds and scents. Here is this lofty and spreading plane-tree, and the agnus castus high and clustering, in the fullest blossom and the greatest fragrance; and the stream which flows beneath the plane-tree is deliciously cold to the feet. Judging from the ornaments and images, this must be a spot sacred to Achelous and the Nymphs. How delightful is the breeze: so very sweet; and there is a sound in the air shrill and summerlike which makes answer to the chorus of the cicadae. But the greatest charm of all is the grass, like a pillow gently sloping to the head. My dear Phaedrus, you have been an admirable guide.

III. Death of Socrates
from *Phaedo*, 3-23-25-28-65-67

Phaedo

As Socrates lay in prison we had been in the habit of assembling early in the morning at the court in which the trial took place, and which is not far from the prison. There we used to wait talking with one another until the opening of the doors (for they were not opened very early); then we went in and generally passed the day with Socrates. On our arrival the jailer who answered the door, instead of admitting us, came out and told us to stay until he called us. He soon returned and said that we might come in. On entering we found Socrates just released from chains, and Xanthippe, whom you know, sitting by him, and holding his child in her arms. Socrates, sitting up on the couch, bent and rubbed his leg, saying, as he was rubbing: "How singular is the thing called pleasure, and how curiously related to pain, which might be thought to be the opposite of it; Why, because each pleasure and pain is a sort of nail which nails and rivets the soul to the body I am not very likely to persuade other men that I do not regard my present situation as a misfortune, if I cannot even persuade you that I am no worse off now than at any other time in my life. Will you not allow that I have as much of the spirit of prophecy in me as the swans? For they, when they perceive that they must die, having sung all their life long, do then sing more lustily than ever, rejoicing in the thought that they are about to go away to the god whose ministers they are."

Often, I have wondered at Socrates, but never more than on that occasion. I was close to him on his right hand, seated on a sort of stool, and he on a couch which was a good deal higher. He stroked my head, and pressed the hair upon my neck—he had a way of playing with my hair; and then he said: "Tomorrow, Phaedo, I suppose that these fair locks of yours will be severed." When he had spoken these words, he arose and went into a chamber to bathe; Crito followed him and told us to wait. When he came out, he sat down with us again after his bath, but not much was said. Soon the jailer, who was the servant of the Eleven, entered and stood by him, saying: "To you, Socrates, whom I know to be the noblest and gentlest and best of all who ever came to this place, I will not impute the angry feelings of other men, who rage and swear at me, when, in obedience to the authorities, I bid them drink the poison—indeed, I am sure that you will not be angry with me; for others, as you are aware, and not I, are to blame. And so fare you well, and try to bear lightly what must needs be—you know my errand." Then bursting into tears he turned away and went out. Socrates looked at him and said: "I return your good wishes, and will do as you bid." Then turning to us, he said: "How charming the man is: since I have been in prison he has always been coming to see me, and at times he would talk to me, and was as good to me as could be, and now see how generously he sorrows on my account. We must do as he says, Crito; and therefore let the cup be brought, if the poison is prepared: if not, let the attendant prepare some."

Crito made a sign to the servant, who was standing by; and he went out, and having been absent for some time, returned with the jailer carrying the cup of poison. Socrates said: "You, my good friend, who are experienced in these matters, shall give me directions how I am to proceed." The man answered: "You have only to walk about until your legs are heavy, and then to lie down, and the poison will act." At the same time he handed the cup to Socrates. Then raising the cup to his lips, quite readily and cheerfully he drank off the poison. And hitherto most of us had been able to control our sorrow; but now when we saw him drinking, and saw too that he had finished the draught, we could no longer forbear, and in spite of myself my own tears were flowing fast; so that I covered my face and wept, not for him, but at the thought of my own calamity in having to part from such a friend. And he walked about until, as he said, his legs began to fail, and then he lay on his back, according to the directions, and the man who gave him the poison now and then looked at his feet and legs; and after a while he pressed his foot hard, and asked him if he could feel; and he said: "No"; and then his leg, and so upwards and upwards, and showed us that he was cold and stiff. And he felt them himself, and said: "When the poison reaches the heart, that will be the end." He was beginning to grow cold about the groin, when he uncovered his face, for he had covered himself up, and said—they were his last words—he said: "Crito, I owe a cock to Asclepius; will you remember to pay the debt?" In a minute or two a movement was heard, and the attendants uncovered him; his eyes were set, and Crito closed his eyes and mouth. Such was the end, Echecrates, of our friend; concerning whom I may truly say, that of all the men of his time whom I have known, he was the wisest and justest and best.

English translation by Benjamin Jowett (1817-1893)